Am I Different?

Written by Johnathan Aubrey
Illustrated by Ben Rowberry

This book is based on my life and experience as a child trying to ride a bike with cerebral palsy (CP). CP is a group of disorders linked to the brain. Cerebral refers to the part of the brain that controls the nervous system: movement, learning, speech, hearing, seeing, and thinking. Palsy refers to the fact that this part of the brain is weak or damaged. People with CP vary in how well they can function ranging from mild, moderate, to severe. CP is caused by lack of brain development or damage before, during, or shortly after birth. It is not hereditary nor contagious and does not get worse or better over time. The brain is like the latest smart phone on the best network with both caller and receiver standing in the best location. A brain with CP is like using walkie-talkies: 10-4.

Copyright © 2023 by Winning Despite Obstacles

All rights reserved. No part of this book may be used or reproduced in any manner whatsoever without written consent and permission from the author except in the case of brief quotations embodied in critical articles and review. For more information on the author or this book see www.WinningDespiteObstacles.com

Library of Congress Control Number: 2023920004

ISBN 979-8-35094-585-0

Dedication

This book is dedicated to those who decide to step up and do hard things. I believe that stepping up to do hard things will inspire and motivate others. I wrote this book to help companies, organizations, and the rising generation create a culture where doing hard things is the norm and inspiring people is a natural occurrence. Special thanks to the contributors of this book: Ben Rowberry, Kimberly Farmer, Karalee Colton, Cheyenne Nielsen, and Charlie Lythgoe. Their hard work and support made this book possible.

"Mommy, am I different?"

"John, everyone is different in some way. Why do you ask?"

"A kid at school asked my name. I told him, but he didn't understand me."

"Oh John, were they mean to you?"

"No, he was nice to me. Most people are. I just wonder why I walk and talk differently than others."

"Sweetie, you were born with cerebral palsy. This makes it more difficult for your muscles to control your body, so you walk and talk differently. But remember, you bring happiness to a lot of people. What else happened today?"

"I had a lot of fun at recess with my friends. I try my best to keep up with everyone, but it's hard."

"I know that you don't like to be left out. That's why Daddy and I have a surprise for Leo, Olivia, and you tonight."

"WOW, a bike with training wheels! Amazing! Can I ride it now?"

"Olivia, watch how fast I can go!"

"Do you want to race?"

"That will be fun! My training wheels will give me a head start, so I am going to win."

"No way! My bike is bigger and faster. On your mark. Get set. Go!"

"**MOMMMMY!** We were racing and Olivia ran over me. It huuurts!"

"Olivia, how did this happen?"

"John got in my way, and we accidentally crashed."

"Oh my! John, let's go clean you up."

"Mom, why doesn't my bike have training wheels anymore? I can't ride it without them."

"Daddy and I think it will be safer for you to ride your tricycle."

I guess people with cerebral palsy can't ride a bike

"We just want to keep you safe. Your brother and friends are riding around outside. Why don't you grab your tricycle and join them?"

I don't feel like doing anything right now. I'm just going to sit on my bed."

"Time out! I need a break."

"John, why do you always sit on a bike when you are too tired from playing tag? You've been doing that for years."

"Leo, I want to ride a bike, but people with cerebral palsy can't."

"SAYS WHO?"

"Well, mom and dad took my bike away after the accident."

"So what? If you want to ride, then do it. It will take more work than just sitting on a bike to learn how to ride."

"Hey Leo, where are you going?"

"Our friends are riding bikes to the pool. See you later!"

This is so **HARD**. I need to get both feet on the pedal and keep my balance.

I'm doing everything I have watched all the other kids do.

I just need to keep trying. I am different, but I can do this!

"I saw you trying to ride your brother's bike today. How is it going?"

"So **HARD**. I think I'm doing what I'm supposed to, but I don't seem to be any closer to riding. I'm so frustrated!"

"Oh John, I understand that not being able to ride a bike has been difficult, but why are you so determined to try when it has been so painful to learn?"

"Because being lonely and bored is **MORE** painful! I am tired of being different. I don't care what anyone says. **I AM** going to ride a bike!"

"Persistence pays off. You'll have to just keep trying. Sweet dreams."

"Sweetie, are you okay, you just face-planted on the road!"

"Mom, I'M FANTASTIC! I just rode a bike! I'M SO EXCITED! Come watch me ride."

"John, it is so magical to watch you ride a bike. Do you know what the best part of this is?"

"Being different doesn't matter. I can **STILL** do hard things!"

"Yes, yes, yes. You can do hard things."